# American Lives

# John Glenn

Elizabeth Raum

**Heinemann Library**
**Chicago, Illinois**

© 2006 Heinemann Library
a division of Reed Elsevier Inc.
Chicago, Illinois

Customer Service 888-454-2279
Visit our website at www.heinemannlibrary.com

Designed by Joanna Hinton-Malivoire and
Q2A Creative

Printed in China by
WKT Company Limited

10 09 08 07 06
10 9 8 7 6 5 4 3 2 1

**Library of Congress Cataloging-in-Publication Data**
Raum, Elizabeth.
  John Glenn / by Elizabeth Raum.-- 1st ed.
     p. cm. -- (American lives)
  Includes bibliographical references and index.
  ISBN 1-4034-6940-7 (hc) -- ISBN 1-4034-6947-4
     (pb)
  1. Glenn, John, 1921---Juvenile literature. 2.
Astronauts--United States--Biography--Juvenile
literature. 3. Legislators--United States--Biography--
Juvenile literature. I. Title. II. Series.

  TL789.85.G6R38 2005

  629.45'0092--dc22

                    2005006253

**Acknowledgments**
The author and publishers are grateful to the
following for permission to reproduce copyright
material: Corbis p. 10; Corbis/Bettmann title page,
pp. 6, 7, 12, 13, 14, 15, 21, 25, 26, 27; Corbis/NASA
pp. 20, 28; Empics/AP p. 24; Getty Images/Time-
Life Pictures p. 22; NASA/Johnson Space Center
cover, pp. 4, 5, 18, 29; NASA/Kennedy Space Center
pp. 5, 19; Rex Features pp. 11, 16; Science Photo
Library p. 17; The John & Annie Glenn Historical
Site pp. 8, 9; World Book Encyclopaedia Science
Service, Inc. p. 23

Every effort has been made to contact copyright
holders of any material reproduced in this book.
Any omissions will be rectified in subsequent
printings if notice is given to the publisher.

The photograph on the cover is an official NASA
photograph of John Glenn.

# Contents

Some words are shown in bold, **like this.** You can find out what they mean by looking in the glossary.

# Liftoff

On February 20, 1962, astronaut John Glenn lay on his back in a tiny space **capsule** named *Friendship 7*. A 65-foot Atlas rocket would blast the tiny capsule into **orbit** around Earth.

John Glenn, in his space suit, is ready for launch.

Glenn listened to the countdown though the headphones in his helmet. At four seconds to liftoff, Glenn felt the rocket come to life, and then he felt a small shudder as the mighty Atlas left Earth.

## Timeline

| 1921 | 1941 | 1943 |
|------|------|------|
| *Born in Cambridge, Ohio* | *Earns pilot's license; joins Navy Air Corps* | *Marries Annie Castor* |

The Atlas pushed Glenn into space at a speed of 17,545 miles (28,236 kilometers) per hour. Glenn was not scared. After years of practice, he was ready to make history.

As a boy, John Glenn had dreamed of flying. He made model airplanes and read about Charles Lindbergh, a famous pilot, and the Wright Brothers, who invented the first airplane. But he never imagined that one day his name would appear in the record books as the first American to orbit Earth.

The Mercury Atlas rocket sends *Friendship 7* into space.

| 1959 | 1962 | 1974 | 1998 |
| --- | --- | --- | --- |
| *Chosen as astronaut* | *Orbits Earth on February 20* | *Elected to Senate* | *Returns to space on Discovery* |

# Childhood

John Hershel Glenn Jr. was born in Cambridge, Ohio, on July 18, 1921. Two years later, his family moved to New Concord, Ohio. They adopted John's sister, Jean. John's mother was a teacher. His father, who was a plumber, often took John on business trips. One day when John was eight, they stopped at an airfield. A pilot offered to fly John and his father over the Ohio countryside.

From that moment on John Glenn was hooked on flying.

This picture shows John Glenn at age four months.

John's parents are shown here standing in front of their Ohio home.

The Glenns attended church every Sunday. They were friends with a couple called the Castors, who had a little girl named Annie. Annie and John played together as babies. As they grew older, they became best friends.

When John was nine or ten he joined the town band and learned to play the trumpet. His father, who had been a soldier in World War I (1914–1918), asked John to play **taps** with him during the Memorial Day service.

## Memorial Day

*Memorial Day is a national holiday held each May to remember men and women who died while serving their country.*

# Ohio Rangers and High School

There was no Boy Scout troop in New Concord, so eleven-year-old John and his friends formed their own club. They called it the Ohio Rangers. They met once a week and talked about sports. They earned money to buy bats, balls, and football helmets so that they could play other teams. They even built a camp in the woods. John spent 60 or 70 nights that summer sleeping at the camp with the Rangers.

A four-year-old John Glenn stands with his little sister Jean in this photo.

John Glenn is seated on the arm of the chair in this picture of the cast of his senior play. John had the leading role.

John was a good student. In high school, he liked science and **civics** best. He worked as a reporter for the school paper and played trumpet in the town band. He played on his school tennis, basketball, and football teams.

John also found time to date Annie Castor. Annie finished high school a year before John. She headed to Muskingum College in New Concord. When John graduated the next year, he decided to go to Muskingum, too.

# Pilot Training

John Glenn learned to fly on a plane similar to this one.

At Muskingum John studied **chemistry**. He also played on the college football team. During his second year of college, John saw a notice for a pilot training program run by the college **physics** department. If he passed, he would get a pilot's license. John signed up.

He learned quickly and got his pilot's license in June 1941, just before he turned 21.

John knew that the United States Army needed pilots to help fight the war in Europe. He listened to reports of the fighting. On December 7, 1941, the United States was attacked at Pearl Harbor. John Glenn talked with Annie and his parents about joining the Army. His parents wanted him to finish college, but John was firm. He wanted to defend his country.

Glenn was a Navy test pilot when this picture was taken.

# Combat Pilot

John signed up for the Army Air Corps. He waited to hear from them, but when no word came, he joined the Navy instead. Before he left New Concord, he asked Annie Castor to marry him. She said yes. They would get married as soon as he finished training.

It was almost six months before John returned to Ohio with his pilot's wings. He married Annie on April 6, 1943.

Glenn is pictured here in uniform. He won many medals as a Navy officer.

The Distinguished Flying Cross was given to Glenn for heroism in battle.

John was eager to fly **combat** missions in the war, but he needed more training. John switched from the Navy to the Marines, and on January 6, 1944, he received orders to go **overseas**. He said goodbye to Annie and left for the Marshall Islands. He flew 59 dive-bombing missions and earned several medals. His **squadron** was ordered back to Maryland, and he was promoted to captain. The war ended in August 1945.

# Korean War and Test Pilot

Three months after the end of the war Glenn became a father. His son David was born on December 13, 1945. Annie and John decided that John should stay in the Marines.

Soon Glenn was sent to China to help keep the peace. He was there when he got the news that his daughter, Lyn, had been born. He also fought in the Korean War (1950–1953). In 1953 he flew 90 missions and earned several more medals for his skill and bravery.

Annie, David, and Lyn greet John after his record-breaking flight.

Next Glenn headed to the Naval Test Pilot School in Maryland. After months of training, he became a test pilot. It was dangerous work, but he loved it.

On July 16, 1957, he flew from California to New York City in 3 hours and 23 minutes at an average speed of 723 miles (1,164 kilometers) per hour. His plane, called the *Silver Bullet*, had beaten the old cross-country speed record by 21 minutes. The

Glenn waves from the *Silver Bullet*.

flight made John Glenn famous. The *New York Times* named him "Man of the Year."

# Astronaut

The Mercury Seven meet the press. John Glenn is standing on the right.

In 1958 the government set up the National Aeronautics and Space Administration (**NASA**) to explore space. NASA invited test pilots to apply to become astronauts. John Glenn applied. He passed many difficult tests and joined the first group of astronauts, called the Mercury Seven. On April 9, 1959, NASA introduced the Mercury Seven astronauts to reporters. John Glenn spoke easily with the press and quickly became a favorite.

## Astronaut

*The word* astronaut *comes from the Greek words* astro *for "star" and* nautes *for "sailor."*

The astronauts trained for months. On May 5, 1961, Alan Shepard became the first American in space. On July 21, 1961, Gus Grissom became the second American in space. Both flights lasted about fifteen minutes. The next astronaut would **orbit** Earth. In November NASA announced that John Glenn was scheduled for the orbital flight. His good friend, the astronaut Scott Carpenter, would be his back-up.

Yuri Gagarin is shown here in his spaceship, *Vostok 1.*

## First Person in Space

*The Russian cosmonaut Yuri Gagarin became the first human being to orbit Earth on April 12, 1961.*

# In Orbit

As **NASA** worked out the details of the flight, Glenn talked to Annie, Dave, and Lyn about the dangers he would face. No American had ever gone into **orbit**. Despite all the careful planning and testing, something could go wrong. Glenn wanted his family to be prepared in case he died in space.

### *Friendship 7*

*Dave and Lyn Glenn helped their father name his spaceship. They chose* Friendship *to show the way Americans felt about other countries and the number 7 for the Mercury Seven astronauts.*

Glenn climbs into *Friendship 7*, preparing for launch.

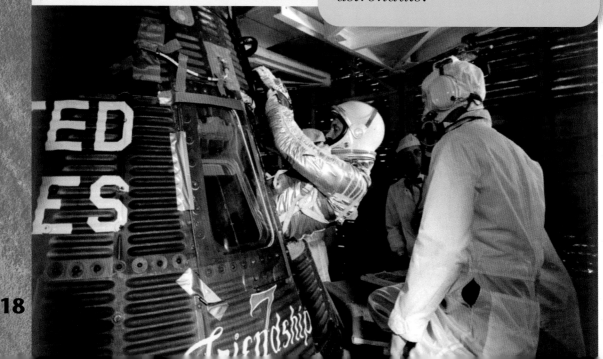

An automatic camera inside *Friendship 7* took this picture of Glenn in space.

Bad weather caused several delays. Finally, on February 20, 1962, John Glenn climbed into his **capsule**, *Friendship 7*. The rocket roared to life and John Glenn was blasted into space. The whole capsule shook. Pressure increased on John Glenn as he left Earth's **gravity** behind. Five minutes into the flight, *Friendship 7* began to orbit Earth. Glenn looked out the small window and saw the Earth far below.

# Re-entry and Celebrations

Glenn took pictures and described the view from space. *Friendship 7* **orbited** Earth at 17,500 miles (28,164 kilometers) per hour. Tracking stations around the world followed its progress. People in Perth and Rockingham, Australia, left their lights on. Glenn spotted them from space and said thank you. After almost five hours in space and three orbits, Glenn fired the rockets that would bring him back to Earth. *Friendship 7* looked like a fireball as it entered Earth's **atmosphere**.

This is the first photo of Earth from space orbit. It was taken by John Glenn.

President Kennedy thanks John Glenn and awards him the Distinguished Service Medal.

A Navy ship waited in the Atlantic to pluck Glenn and the *Friendship 7* out of the ocean. After two days of talks with **NASA** and the other astronauts, John Glenn returned to Florida. One hundred thousand people lined the roadway. President John Kennedy welcomed Glenn and gave him the NASA Distinguished Service medal. People in New York City, New Concord, Ohio, and Washington, D.C., held parades in his honor. John Glenn was a real American hero.

# Politics

Speaking to Congress and meeting President Kennedy reminded John Glenn of his interest in **civics**. Both President Kennedy and his brother, Robert Kennedy, told Glenn that he could serve his country as a **senator** from Ohio.

On January 17, 1964, Glenn announced that he would run for the Senate. A few weeks later, he slipped and hit his head on the bathtub. He suffered an inner ear injury that made him dizzy. He had to quit the race.

John Glenn receives a hero's welcome in New York City.

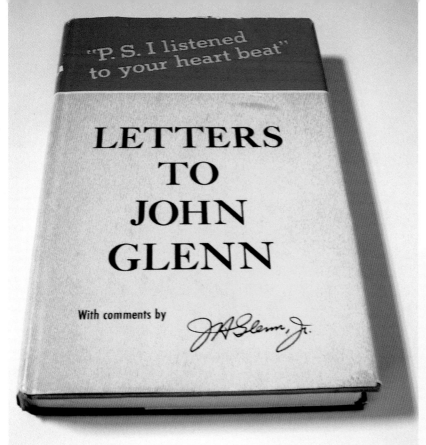

This is the cover of John Glenn's book, *P.S. I Listened to Your Heart Beat.*

Glenn got better after spending two months in the hospital and several more months recovering at home. He **retired** from the Marines and took a job with Royal Crown Cola. He visited many countries around the world. Like his father, John Glenn was curious and loved to learn new things. Other people were curious about him, too, so he wrote a book called *P.S. I Listened to Your Heart Beat.* It included letters people had written to him.

# Senator

The Glenns had a busy life. Both children were in college, so John and Annie Glenn moved to New York City. They met interesting people and tried new things.

In 1970, Glenn ran for the Senate again. It was a close race, but he lost. He learned what

John Glenn is pictured here during his run for the U.S. Senate in 1974.

to do better the next time, and in 1974 he won. John Glenn worked hard in the Senate and served on several **committees.**

In 1976, President Jimmy Carter asked Glenn if he would like to be vice president. Glenn thought about it. He liked the idea, but Carter chose someone else instead. John Glenn began to think of running for president himself.

In the meantime, Glenn served on the Senate Foreign Relations Committee. This committee deals with how the United States works with other countries. John Glenn was proud of the plan he helped to develop for stopping the spread of **nuclear weapons.**

John Glenn watches President Carter sign the nuclear weapons bill.

# Patriot

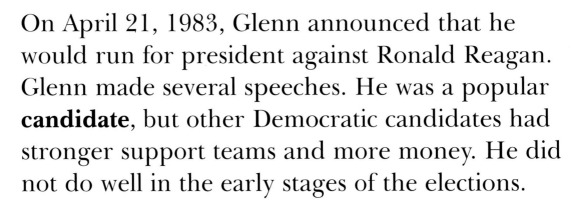

On April 21, 1983, Glenn announced that he would run for president against Ronald Reagan. Glenn made several speeches. He was a popular **candidate**, but other Democratic candidates had stronger support teams and more money. He did not do well in the early stages of the elections.

Even though many people thought he would be a good president, Glenn dropped out of the race. However, his defeat did not discourage him from being a **politician**.

Glenn runs for president in 1984.

As a senator, Glenn always supported the space program.

Glenn served a total of four **terms** as the senator from Ohio. He tried to end wasteful government spending and to promote science. He encouraged the Senate to support **NASA** and space exploration.

On February 20, 1997, Glenn announced that he would not run again. He had spent 24 years as a senator.

# Back into Space

Glenn takes a break from flight training to sign autographs for students.

While in the Senate, Glenn served on the Special **Committee** on Aging. As he read reports, he noticed that many changes that happen when people get older also happen to astronauts in space. He wondered if sending an older person into space would help scientists. If so, John Glenn, age 77, was ready to go. **NASA** agreed that it was important research. On January 16, 1998, NASA announced that Glenn would return to space as a **payload specialist**.

Glenn's space flights were 36 years apart.

Glenn met the space shuttle *Discovery* crew and trained for the mission. He performed medical tests on himself to see how older people's bodies act in space.

After months of training, the crew was ready. They lifted off on October 29, 1998. John Glenn became the oldest astronaut ever to go into space. The experiments he completed gave doctors useful information about aging and space travel.

Whether young or old, John Glenn served his country as a real American hero.

## John Glenn Firsts

*John Glenn was the first American to orbit the Earth and the first astronaut to return to space when he was an older person.*

# Glossary

**atmosphere**   air surrounding Earth

**candidate**   someone running for political office

**capsule**   closed space designed to protect a person

**chemistry**   science that studies what things are made of and the changes they go through

**civics**   study of local and national government and the duties and the rights of citizens

**combat**   battle

**committee**   group of people working together

**gravity**   force that draws things toward Earth

**NASA**   National Aeronautics and Space Administration, the agency that studies and carries out work in space

**nuclear weapons**   powerful bombs and missiles

**orbit**   move or circle around something

**overseas**   across the sea; to another country

**payload specialist**   astronaut who does experiments

**physics**   science that studies energy and matter

**politician**   person who holds an elected office

**promote**   give a more important job

**retire**   stop working

**senator**   elected representative who serves in the United States Senate

**squadron**   military group

**taps**   bugle call to honor soldiers killed in battle

**term**   time in office (six years for a senator)

# More Books to Read

Bredeson, Carmen. *John Glenn: Space Pioneer.* Brookfield, Conn.: Millbrook Press, 2000.

Streissguth, Thomas. *John Glenn.* Mankato, Minn.: Bridgestone, 2003.

# Places to Visit

**NASA Glenn Visitor Center**
21000 Brookpark Road
Cleveland, Ohio 44135
Phone: 216-433-2001

**National Air and Space Museum**
Independence Ave at 4th Street, SW
Washington, DC 20560
Phone: 202-633-1000
www.nasm.si.edu

# Index